THE ULTIMATE ELVIS QUIZ AND FACT BOOK

QUESTIONS AND FACTS ON THE KING OF ROCK 'N' ROLL

Complied by Scott Stevenson

UNOFFICIAL AND UNAUTHORISED

APEX PUBLISHING LTD

First published in 2015, updated in 2016 by
Apex Publishing Ltd
12A St. John's Road, Clacton on Sea, Essex, CO15 4BP, United Kingdom

www.apexpublishing.co.uk

British Library Cataloguing-in-Publication Data
A catalogue record for this book
is available from the British Library

ISBN 978-1-78538-483-7

Typeset in 12pt Baskerville Win95BT

Production Manager: Chris Cowlin
Cover Design: Hannah Blamires

Publishers Note:
The views and opinions expressed in this publication are those of the author and are not necessarily those of Apex Publishing Ltd

CONTENTS

INTRODUCTION

Elvis Presley was born in Tupelo, Mississippi on 8 January 1935 and raised by a humble, working class family where he was close to both of his parents but particularly his mother, Gladys. He experienced a meteoric rise to fame in the mid-1950s and became possibly the biggest name in rock and roll history, breaking records and girls' hearts along the way. With a huge back catalogue of groundbreaking music, his gorgeous looks and a long list of acting credits, Elvis soon gathered a global fan base. After years in the spotlight, he battled drug addiction and rapid weight gain, coupled with media scrutiny and personal relationship problems, which sadly lead to his untimely death, aged just 42. Today, Elvis is still one of music's most popular icons, with his daughter Lisa Marie and ex-wife Priscilla continuing to ensure that his legacy lives on. This book is intended for Elvis fans to challenge themselves on his incredible life and learn more about their musical hero.

www.apexpublishing.co.uk

QUESTIONS: PERSONAL LIFE

1. Thirty-five minutes before Elvis was born, his mother gave birth to his identical twin brother who was sadly stillborn. What name did they give him?

2. What was the name of Elvis' stepmother who married Elvis' dad, Vernon, in 1960 following the death of his mother in 1958?

3. What was the name of the portly, cigar-smoking manager who represented Elvis for more than 20 years?

4. What was the name of Elvis' beloved mother, who passed away in 1958, aged 46?

5. Who was Elvis engaged to at the time of his death?

6. What was the name of the 'Miss Clairol #51D' colour hair dye that Elvis famously used?

7. Why did Elvis get fired from his Loew's State Movie Theatre usher's job in Memphis when he was a teenager?

8. In what year did Elvis make his first television appearance, with Jackie Gleason stating, "The kid has no right behaving like a sex maniac on a national show"?

9.   Elvis paid $4 to Sun Studio to record his first ever songs as a gift to his mother. *My Happiness* was one, what was the other?

10. What was the name of the road in Tupelo Where Elvis was born?

11. What name did Elvis give to his *Covair 880* jet that he bought in 1975?

12. According to his associate, Byron Raphael, Elvis had a one-night stand with which iconic movie star in 1956?

13. Elvis had a brief affair with which Swedish-American actress and singer after they met during the making of *Viva Las Vegas* in 1964?

14. What was significant about Lisa Marie's birth date (1 February 1968)?

15. Six months after Elvis' separation from Priscilla, he began a relationship with which songwriter, actress and beauty queen?

16. Which actress who left Hollywood to become a Benedictine nun did Elvis have a brief relationship with during the filming of his second movie *Loving You*?

17. What was the name of the high school that Elvis graduated from on 3 June 1953?

18. What was the name of Elvis' date at his senior prom in 1953?

19. Elvis briefly dated which actress who starred in the film *Junior Bonner* along with her then-boyfriend Steve McQueen?

20. At his funeral, Elvis had five pallbearers; Joe Esposito, Billy Smith, Lamar Fike and Dr. George Nichopoulos were four, who was the fifth?

ANSWERS: PERSONAL LIFE

1. Jesse Garon
2. Dee Stanley
3. Colonel Tom Parker
4. Gladys Presley
5. Ginger Alden
6. Black Velvet
7. Using his charm, he would acquire free candy from a female co-worker
8. 1956
9. That's When Your Heartaches Begin
10. Old Saltillo Road (Now Elvis Presley Drive)
11. Lisa Marie
12. Marilyn Monroe
13. Ann-Margret
14. It was exactly nine months to the day that Elvis and Priscilla had married
15. Linda Thompson

16. Dolores Hart
17. Humes High School
18. Regis Wilson
19. Barbara Leigh
20. Charlie Hodge

QUESTIONS:
SINGLES FROM THE 1950s

21. Released in 1956, which single became Elvis' first to sell more than one million copies and is based on a note left by a man who committed suicide in a Florida Hotel?

22. What single, released in 1957, was accompanied by the first ever music video?

23. Elvis had the bestselling single of the 1950s. What was it called?

24. What song was released in 1959 as a double A-side along with 'A Fool Such as I'?

25. Elvis covered and released which song in 1956, originally recorded by Clyde McPhatter and the newly-formed Drifters. It was also covered by Eddie Cochran (1959), Little Richard (1964) and The Jackson 5 (1971)?

26. Which Little Richard song, combining elements of boogie, gospel and blues, did Elvis cover and include on his *Elvis Presley* album. The same song also featured in the T. Rex and Elton John 1972 film Born to Boogie?

27. Released in 1958 and accompanied by 'Don' cha Think It's Time' as a B-side, what song written by Bert Carroll and Russell Moody peaked at number 2 in the American Pop Charts breaking a string of 10 consecutive number 1 hits for Elvis?

28. What song, that Elvis received a rare song writing credit for, was released in 1956 and appeared as the last song on side 1 of the album *Elvis*?

29. Which Arthur Gunter song was covered by Elvis and has a line in the song that refers to his custom-painted 1955 Pink Cadillac that was the band's mode of transport at the time?

30. Sid Wayne and Bix Reichner wrote which 1959 release that gave Elvis the 'hi-fi high and the lights down low'?

31. Released in 1958, this was Elvis' 11th number 1 hit in the United States and was accompanied by 'I Beg of You' as a B-side?

32. In which 1957 release, that has 'Playing For Keeps' as a B-side, does Elvis complain that all his money is being spent excessively?

33. Which 1937 song, written by Thomas A. Dorsey, did Elvis include on his first Christmas album in 1957 with backing by The Jordanaires after hearing them sing it with Eddy Arnold in 1955?

34. Which hit, made popular by Bill Hayley and His Comets in 1954, did Elvis release in 1956 with Scotty Moore, Bill Black and D. J. Fontana providing the music and chorus vocals?

35. What song, released in 1959, featuring a triple negative in the lyrics became the UK's 1000th number 1 single after its second release in 2005?

36. Shaken up after a near-death experience on a flight to Nashville, Elvis and his band tried unsuccessfully to record a song 17 times before being sent away by RCA producer Steve Scholes. Unhappy with the time and money wasted on the session, coupled with Elvis' busy touring schedule, Scholes managed to mix parts from different takes and produced which successful 1956 release?

37. What was the first single recorded and released by Elvis?

38. Which successful Elvis song from 1957 did Billy Joel cover in 1991 for the movie *Honeymoon in Vegas*?

39. What well-known single, originally recorded by Carl Perkins in 1955, was the first song on the groundbreaking album *Elvis Presley*?

40. Which 1955 single with 'Mystery Train' as its B-side was the first recording to make Elvis a nationally known country music star?

ANSWERS:
SINGLES FROM THE 1950s

21. Heartbreak Hotel

22. Jailhouse Rock

23. Hound Dog/Don't be Cruel (1956)

24. I Need Your Love Tonight

25. Money Honey

26. Tutti Frutti

27. Wear My Ring Around Your Neck

28. Paralyzed

29. Baby Let's Play House

30. I Need Your Love Tonight

31. Don't

32. Too Much

33. Peace in the Valley

34. Shake, Rattle and Roll

35. One Night ('I ain't never did no wrong')

36. I Want You, I Need You, I Love You

37. That's All Right (1954)

38. All Shook Up

39. Blue Suede Shoes

40. I Forgot to Remember to Forget

QUESTIONS: MOVIE CAREER

41. Kurt Russell made his film debut aged 11 in which Elvis film?

42. When he was filming *Kid Galahad* in 1961, Elvis thought his chair with 'Mr. Presley' printed on the back was a little too formal and so he had it changed to what?

43. What was the name of Elvis' character in the film *Double Trouble*?

44. Which of Elvis' films was the only one to be nominated for a Golden Globe Award?

45. What film, released in 1969, was Elvis' only movie to not feature him singing on screen?

46. Elvis played stock car driver, Steve Grayson, alongside Nancy Sinatra in which 1968 movie?

47. What was the name of Elvis' final fiction film that dealt with several social issues including romance with the clergy, rape and autism?

48. *Eight Elvises* is a silkscreen painting by American artist Andy Warhol that fetched $100 million at auction in 2008. The original images were taken from a publicity still from which movie?

49. In what film did Elvis play the part of Danny Fisher?

50. Besides *Blue Hawaii*, which other of Elvis' films features the word 'Hawaii'?

51. Complete the title of a 1966 Elvis film, *Frankie and...*?

52. What was the only one of Elvis' movies that didn't make a profit?

53. *Café Europa* was the working title for which movie and remained the official title in a number of European countries?

54. In what movie did Jana Lund give Elvis his very first on-screen kiss?

55. Elvis played Josh Morgan and then donned a blonde wig to also play his hillbilly cousin, Jodie Tatum, in which 1964 movie?

56. In what film did veteran actor Charles Bronson play boxing trainer Lew Nyack?

57. What actress was tragically killed in a car crash soon after she filmed her final scenes as the leading lady in *Jailhouse Rock*?

58. What veteran actress played Elvis' mother in *Blue Hawaii* despite being just 10 years older than him in real life?

59. In what movie does Elvis play a character named Ted who works as a nightclub singer as well as a deep-sea diver searching for gold aboard a sunken ship?

60. Elvis' character, an heir to an oil fortune, swaps places with a water-ski instructor to see if people like him for who he is and not just his money in which 1967 movie?

ANSWERS: MOVIE CAREER

41. *It Happened at the World's Fair* (1963)

42. 'Just Plain Ol' Elvis'

43. Guy Lambert

44. *Girls! Girls! Girls!*

45. *Charro!*

46. *Speedway*

47. *Change of Habit* (1969)

48. *Flaming Star*

49. *King Creole*

50. *Paradise, Hawaiian Style*

51. *Johnny*

52. *Wild in the Country* (1961)

53. *G. I. Blues*

54. *Loving You* (1957). It is a myth that Dolores Hart shared his first kiss; she was in fact his third!

55. *Kissin' Cousins*

56. *Kid Galahad*

57. Judy Tyler

58. Angela Lansbury

59. *Easy Come, Easy Go*

60. *Clambake*

QUESTIONS:
ELVIS AND PRISCILLA

61. In what year did Elvis and Priscilla marry?

62. What was the name of the karate instructor that Elvis thought about having killed following an affair with Priscilla?

63. What actor and school friend of Elvis who wrote the book *Elvis: What Happened* was famously turned away from Elvis and Priscilla's wedding even though he was personally invited and was a member of the Memphis Mafia?

64. Elvis and Priscilla's wedding cake was famously made up of how many tiers?

65. Priscilla was born with the surname Wagner, but she often used the surname of her stepfather during her childhood and adolescence. What was it?

66. Priscilla Presley is thought to have copied which legendary actress' hairstyle, who reportedly turned down a proposal from Elvis?

67. What is the name of Priscilla's autobiography that was published in 1985?

68. In what year did Elvis and Priscilla divorce?

69. Priscilla turned down a role playing one of the three main females in which successful television show?

70. In what year did Priscilla give birth to Lisa Marie?

71. Priscilla set up a celebrity clothing boutique with her friend, Olivia Bis, that was regularly frequented by the likes of Barbra Streisand and Cher. What was it called?

72. What is the name of the Italian-American film director and producer who was in a long-term relationship with Priscilla between 1984 and 2006?

73. How old was Priscilla when she first met Elvis in Germany?

74. When Elvis left Germany in 1960, Priscilla thought she would never see him again. Her fears seemed confirmed when various media outlets reported that he was in a new relationship with which singer and actress, daughter of another very famous singer and actor?

75. Why did the judge in Elvis and Priscilla's divorce court hearing claim it seemed more like a marriage ceremony?

76. Where did Elvis and Priscilla enjoy their honeymoon?

77. What is the name of the corporate entity set up by Priscilla and Elvis' dad, Vernon, to manage the licensing of Elvis related products, music, video content and assets including Graceland?

78. What was Elvis and Priscilla's first wedding dance song?

79. Priscilla played the character Jenna Wade in which popular prime-time soap opera?

80. What was the name of the hotel where Elvis married Priscilla?

ANSWERS: ELVIS AND PRISCILLA

61. 1967 (1 May)
62. Mike Stone

63. Robert 'Red' West

64. Six

65. Beaulieu

66. Tura Satana

67. *Elvis and Me*

68. 1973

69. *Charlie's Angels*

70. 1968

71. Bis & Beau

72. Marco Garibaldi

73. 14

74. Nancy Sinatra

75. Because during the hearing and when leaving the court they were hand in hand

76. Palm Springs, California

77. Elvis Presley Enterprises (EPE)

78. Love Me Tender

79. *Dallas*

80. Aladdin Hotel

QUESTIONS: POT LUCK

81. What was the name of Elvis' hard-drinking pet chimpanzee, rumoured to have been poisoned by a maid who he'd bitten?

82. Showing off his karate moves in his hotel suite in Las Vegas, Elvis broke a bone in which part of a woman's body?

83. Elvis came fifth in a children's talent show when he was ten, singing which song?

84. *Preseucolia imallshookupis* is a species of which insect, named after the Elvis hit?

85. What song, written by Alex North and Hy Zaret, did Elvis only perform during the last year of his life?

86. What was Elvis' dad Vernon's middle name?

87. Elvis only performed two concerts outside of the United States, both were in which country?

88. What film was reportedly in Elvis' VHS player when he died?

89. What did Elvis claim was his favourite soft drink and rumoured to be the inspiration for 'All Shook Up'?

90. What eye condition was Elvis diagnosed with in the 1970s?

91. What singer heard Elvis' song 'It's Now or Never' on the radio whilst in jail and later credited the moment for turning his life around and dedicating it to music?

92. Elvis played the piano and sang which song to family and friends at Graceland on 15 August 1977. Thought to be his last performed song?

93. What book was Elvis reported to be halfway through reading at the time of his death?

94. What collective name was given to Elvis' entourage?

95. What feline name did Elvis give himself whilst singing locally as a teenager?

96. What was the name of the gospel quartet that Elvis auditioned for in 1954 – and was turned down?

97. In 1970, Elvis stated that his two favourite books were *The Impersonal Life* by Joseph S. Benner and which other?

98. How many Grammy Awards did Elvis win?

99. Which well-known singer born David Jones in 1947 shares his birthday with Elvis?

100. Andreas Cornelis van Kuijk was better known by which name?

ANSWERS: POT LUCK

81. Scatter

82. Her ankle

83. Old Shep

84.   Wasp

85.   Unchained Melody

86.   Elvis

87.   Canada

88.   *Monty Python and the Holy Grail*

89.   Pepsi Cola

90.   Glaucoma

91.   Barry White

92.   Blue Eyes Crying in the Rain

93.   *A Scientific Search for the Face of Jesus* by Frank O Adams

94.   The Memphis Mafia

95.   The Hillbilly Cat

96.   The Songfellows

97.   *The Holy Bible*

98.   Three

99.   David Bowie

100. Colonel Tom Parker

QUESTIONS:
SINGLES FROM THE 1960s

101. What song from 1961 is set to the melody of the 18th century French love song 'Plaisir D'Amour'?

102. Elvis had the bestselling single of the 1960s. What was it called?

103. One of Elvis' most recognisable songs (although he never played it live), which song has appeared in countless films and television shows due to its reference to a popular American city?

104. Which 1962 Elvis song, covered by Chris Isaak for his 2011 album Beyond the Sun, featured 'Just Tell Her Jim Said Hello' on the B-side?

105. What song released in 1969 was performed as a duet with Lisa Marie Presley using archive footage of Elvis at a 20th anniversary tribute concert in 1997?

106. One of the bestselling singles of all time, which 1961 release is an adaption of the 1902 Neapolitan ballad 'Torna a Surriento' by Giambattista and Ernesto de Curtis?

107. In what song, his first hit single following his two-year stint in the army, does Elvis talk of wild horses, a grizzly bear and a tiger?

108. What was the B-side to Good Luck Charm, and has also been released by Billy 'Crash' Craddock and Bobby Solo?

109. Elvis' final number 1 single in the United States before his death, which 'mistrusting' 1969 release was written and originally recorded by American songwriter Mark James?

110. 'Hey Memphis', a successful song recorded by rhythm and blues singer LaVern Baker, has the same melody as which 1961 single in which Elvis talks of two female siblings?

111. Written by Victor Young and Edward Heyman and nominated for the Academy Award for Best Song in 1945, which song did Elvis release in 1966 and include as the first track on his twelfth studio album?

112. What song, originally written and performed by Ray Charles, did Elvis release as a single in 1963?

113. Featuring in Disney's 2002 animated movie Lilo & Stitch, which Gold certified 1963 release includes the vocals of J. D. Sumner portraying the voice of Satan?

114. What song originally recorded and written by Chuck Willis in 1953 was released in 1961 as a double A-side along with 'Wild in the Country'?

115. What song, recorded just weeks after the assassinations of Bobby Kennedy and Martin Luther King Jr. in 1968, is notable for using direct quotations from King's speeches as lyrics?

116. Written by Roy Turk and Lou Handman and containing a spoken word section based on a line from William Shakespeare's *As You Like It*, which song was recorded many times during the 1920s before Colonel Tom Parker convinced Elvis to record it, stating that it was his wife's favourite love song?

117. Written by Artie Glen for his teenage son, Darrell, to record, which song also recorded by Bob Marley & The Wailers did Elvis cover and release as an 'Easter Special' in April 1965?

118. In what 1962 release does Elvis mention a four-leaf clover, an old horseshoe and a rabbit's foot on a string?

119. What song that features a girl's name in the title did Elvis release just a couple of months after Del Shannon recorded the same song for his album *Runaway With Del Shannon*?

120. What release, which includes a picture of a broken heart on the sleeve, was the only non-movie song in a 28-month period during the 1960s and appeared as the B-side to 'Kissin' Cousins'?

ANSWERS:
SINGLES FROM THE 1960s

101. Can't Help Falling In Love

102. It's Now or Never

103. Viva Las Vegas

104. She's Not You

105. Don't Cry Daddy

106. Surrender

107. Stuck on You

108. Anything That's Part of You

109. Suspicious Minds

110. Little Sister

111. Love Letters

112. What'd I Say

113. (You're The) Devil in Disguise

114. I Feel So Bad

115. If I Can Dream

116. Are You Lonesome Tonight?

117. Crying in the Chapel

118. Good Luck Charm

119. (Marie's the Name) His Latest Flame

120. It Hurts Me

QUESTIONS:
MOVIE SOUNDTRACKS

121. Which popular, cuddly number 1 hit, released in 1957 was written by Kal Mann and Bernie Lowe and recorded for Elvis' second motion picture *Loving You*?

122. Which soundtrack album is not only Elvis' most successful chart album but also the number 1 album of 1961, having stayed at the top spot for 20 consecutive weeks?

123. What song, an adaptation of the Civil War song 'Aura Lee', was the title song of Elvis' movie debut in 1956?

124. 'Relax', 'Take Me to the Fair' and 'Cotton Candy Land' appear on which soundtrack album?

125. In which film did Elvis sing 'One Track Heart'?

126. What album that accompanies a film set in the 19th century, features songs originating from that time period including 'When the Saints Go Marching In' and 'Down by the Riverside'?

127. Recorded for Elvis' first post-Army movie, which soundtrack remained on the Billboard album chart for a total of 111 weeks, the longest of any album in Elvis' career?

128. What song that featured in the film *G. I. Blues*, contains two parts in German?

129. 'I'm Yours' featured in which 1965 movie?

130. Which two-word rhyming soundtrack that features two Elvises on the sleeve cover, was released on 1 June, 1967 – the same day as The Beatles' landmark album *Sgt. Pepper's Lonely Hearts Club Band*?

131. Which song from the film *Live a Little, Love a Little* was remixed and featured in the 2001 film Ocean's Eleven?

132. What soundtrack album with a Mexican theme was released in 1963 and features a version of the 1937 mariachi song 'Guadalajara'?

133. What song from *Girl Happy* was recorded in the same year (1964) by Bill Haley & His Comets but under the different title 'Yeah, She's Evil'?

134. 'Hard Headed Woman' was a number 1 single that became the first rock and roll single to earn the RIAA designation of Gold Record. It was recorded as part of the soundtrack for which movie?

135. What was Elvis' final film to have a full soundtrack album and also the last to be released in both stereo and mono, making the rare mono version a sought-after item among collectors?

136. What song that features prominently in the film *Jailhouse Rock* includes Elvis requesting to have his back scratched?

137. The title song from which soundtrack was taken from the 1937 Bing Crosby film *Waikiki Wedding*?

138. 'Kismet', 'Mirage' and 'Golden Coins' appear on which 1965 soundtrack, which also features Elvis on the album sleeve with camels and palm trees in the background?

139. In which film did Elvis perform the song 'Return to Sender'?

140. Which single from the movie *Blue Hawaii* was released as a double A-side with 'Can't Help Falling in Love' and is a mix of Hawaiian folk music and rock and roll?

ANSWERS: MOVIE SOUNDTRACKS

121. (Let Me Be Your) Teddy Bear
122. *Blue Hawaii*
123. *Love Me Tender*
124. *It Happened at the World's Fair*
125. *Roustabout*
126. *Frankie and Johnny*
127. *G. I. Blues*

128. Wooden Heart

129. *Tickle Me*

130. *Double Trouble*

131. A Little Less Conversation

132. *Fun in Acapulco*

133. The Meanest Girl in Town

134. *King Creole*

135. *Speedway*

136. Treat Me Nice

137. *Blue Hawaii*

138. *Harum Scarum*

139. *Girls! Girls! Girls!*

140. Rock-A-Hula Baby

QUESTIONS:
SINGLES FROM THE 1970s

141. In 1972, Elvis had his last U.S. top 10 hit during his lifetime with which hot song?

142. What song made famous by Dusty Springfield in 1966 did Elvis release in 1970 and include on his album *That's the Way It Is*?

143. Elvis recorded which critically appreciated song (originally by Gwen McCrae) in March 1972 dropping the 'You Were' from the beginning of the title?

144. Originally released by Ray Peterson and covered by The Platters, Elvis recorded which track live in concert in Las Vegas, becoming one of the most successful records in the UK ever?

145. Which song with a four-letter title was written by Shirl Milete and released as the last song on Love Letters from Elvis?

146. Which single from an album of the same name was originally written by Chuck Berry to the melody of American folk song 'Wabash Cannonball' and featured in the 1997 movie Men in Black?

147. Made famous by Les Paul and Mary Ford in 1953, which song has been covered many times including Jerry Lee Lewis for his album *Mean Old Man* and was sung by John Travolta in the 2004 movie *A Love Song for Bobby Long*?

148. The last single released before Elvis' death, on what appropriately named song does J. D. Sumner sing an incredible double low 'C' note at the end of each chorus?

149. What song recorded in 1973 and included on the *Good Times* album is sung in a first person narrative from the point of view of a father explaining to his young sleeping son the loveless relationship that he is in with the child's mother?

150. A story of someone going from tattered clothes to being a millionaire made famous following Tony Bennett's 1953 version, what song did Elvis announce he was to sing towards the end of a concert on New Year's Eve 1976 to the surprise of his unpractised band members?

151. One of the most recorded songs of the 20th century and nominated for an Oscar in 1955, what song made popular by The Righteous Brothers in 1965 was recorded by Elvis but released after his death in 1978?

152. What festive hit at 7 minutes 20 seconds in length and originally recorded by Johnny Moore's Three Blazers in 1947 did Elvis include on his 1971 album Elvis sings *The Wonderful World of Christmas*?

153. In what 1970 song does Elvis passionately sing about a lover searching for his lady in a bluegrass downpour?

154. Which song that Elvis covered in 1972 was a major international hit for Roberta Flack, winning her the Grammy Award for Record and Song of the Year 1972?

155. Made popular by Jack Greene in 1966, in which 1971 Elvis song does the narrator talk of losing all of his possessions?

156. Which parody written by James Taylor that mentions a napalm bomb did Elvis add to his concert repertoire and perform right up until his final concert?

157. Written by Canadian singer-songwriter Buffy Sainte-Marie and covered by many artists including Neil Diamond, Barbra Streisand and Andy Williams, which 1972 song tells the tale of two lovers who can't be together due to their differing backgrounds?

158. Adapting the 1967 French pop song 'Comme d'habitude', Paul Anka wrote which popular song for Frank Sinatra that Elvis covered and performed in concert even though Anka didn't think it suited his style?

159. Recorded in the Jungle Room at Graceland in 1976 and sitting at number 1 in the charts just six months before Elvis died, which song was released with a limited edition pressed in an appropriate translucent blue vinyl?

160. In which 1970 release does Elvis sing about his mother enjoying growing certain flowers in her garden?

ANSWERS:
SINGLES FROM THE 1970s

141. Burning Love

142. You Don't Have to Say You Love Me

143. Always on My Mind

144. The Wonder of You

145. Life

146. Promised Land

147. I Really Don't Want to Know

148. Way Down

149. My Boy

150. Rags to Riches

151. Unchained Melody

152. Merry Christmas Baby

153. Kentucky Rain

154. The First Time Ever I Saw Your Face

155. There Goes My Everything

156. Steamroller Blues

157. Until It's Time for You to Go

158. My Way

159. Moody Blue

160. Mama Liked the Roses

QUESTIONS:
MORE POT LUCK

161. Which 1973 Television special drew in more viewers than the moon landings?

162. What was the name of Elvis' grandmother who lived at Graceland?

163. The death of which legendary comedian was somewhat overshadowed by Elvis' death as it came just three days later?

164. What James Bond film is thought to be the last film Elvis watched at a cinema?

165. In 1973, Elvis gave boxer Muhammad Ali a white robe with which two words emblazoned across the back, what were they?

166. A type of which traditional pattern (made up of pink, baby blue, black and gold) was created in 2007 for the 30th anniversary of Elvis' death?

167. What was the only country in the UK that Elvis stepped foot in?

168. Who was President of the United States at the time of Elvis' death, coincidently one of his distant cousins?

169. When one journalist called Elvis 'The King of Rock and Roll', Elvis replied that the moniker should instead be given to which singer?

170. What did Johnny Carson apparently call Elvis on *The Tonight Show*, which angered him so much that he refused to watch again?

171. Which American businessman and media entrepreneur bought an 85% stake in Elvis Presley Enterprises in 2005?

172. What type of animal was Elvis' pet that he named Bowtie?

173. What film, directed by Allan Arkush, is an exaggerated account of Elvis' meeting with a United States President in 1970?

174. Elvis gave his entourage gold and diamond rings with the imprinted letters T. C. B. What did this stand for?

175. What animal was Elvis' karate name?

176. In 1958, Elvis left New York for Germany to serve in the United States Army on which ship?

177. Elvis recorded 21 songs with what colour in the title?

178. What animal was Elvis in Chinese astrology?

179. Just before he died, Elvis commissioned his stage electrician to design a version of his white jumpsuit that could do what?

180. Which Welsh singer stated in 2009 that Elvis had serenaded him as he was taking a shower backstage in Las Vegas?

ANSWERS: MORE POT LUCK

161. Aloha From Hawaii

162. Minnie Mae Presley

163. Groucho Marx

164. *The Spy Who Loved Me* (1977)

165. People's Choice

166. Tartan

167. Scotland (his military plane landed to refuel at Glasgow's Prestwick airport on his trip from Germany back to the United States. He had two hours at the airport before re-boarding)

168. Jimmy Carter

169. Fats Domino

170. Forty and fat

171. Robert Sillerman

172. *A turkey*

173. *Elvis Meets Nixon*

174. Take Care of Business

175. Tiger

176. USS General George M. Randall

177. Blue (Blue Suede Shoes, Moody Blue, Blue Christmas, G. I. Blues, Indescribably Blue, Blue Moon of Kentucky, Steamroller Blues, Blue Moon, Good Time Charlie's Got the Blues,

Milkcow Blues Boogie, Something Blue, Blue River, A Mess of Blues, When My Blue Moon Turns to Gold Again, Blue Hawaii, Mean Woman Blue, I'm Gonna Bid My Blues Goodbye, Beach Boy Blue, Blue Eyes Crying in The Rain, I've Been Blue, Steamroller Blues)

178.   A dog

179.   Shoot laser beams into the audience

180.   Tom Jones

QUESTIONS: ALBUMS

WORK OUT THE ELVIS ALBUM FROM THE CLUES BELOW

181.   Released on 8 April 1960, this was Elvis' 10th Studio album and marked his return to recording following his discharge from the army. The front cover appropriately shows Elvis in front of a blue stage curtain wearing an army trench coat and the inside features photographs from his army career. It represented a new sound for Elvis, moving towards pop music and his first album to be recorded in stereo. The album featured fan-favourite 'Soldier Boy' and a cover of Peggy Lee's 'Fever'?

182. Earning Elvis his second of three Grammy Awards, this 1972 contemporary gospel album was certified platinum in 1999 by the RIAA. The mostly black album cover shows Elvis singing into a microphone and it features such hits as 'Amazing Grace' and 'A Thing Called Love'?

183. A live album taken from a 1973 concert in Hawaii, this show was aired in over 40 countries across Europe and Asia. The album was Elvis' final number 1 during his lifetime and remains the biggest selling album released in quadraphonic sound. The album cover shows the Earth from space and Elvis wearing his trademark white American eagle jumpsuit and the set-list features a compilation of some of his greatest hits?

184. Released on 16 June 1971, this album was created using tracks from a recording session in 1970 that weren't used on previous albums. The album's title track was previously recorded and released as a single in 1966 and the track 'Got My Mojo Working' was included from an impromptu jam session. Other hits on the album include 'Life', 'Sylvia' and 'Heart of Rome'?

185. A compilation album of tracks including 'Your Cheatin' Heart', which was originally released 19 years beforehand. It was released by RCA in early 1977, just months before Elvis' death and the album's title track was made famous by country singer Jim Reeves?

186. Released in 1970, this was Elvis' 40th album. Consisting of eight studio tracks and four live songs from a concert in Las Vegas, the album accompanied a documentary of the same name. Tracks included covers of 'Bridge Over Troubled Water' and 'You've Lost That Lovin' Feelin''?

187. Elvis' final studio album released the month before his death and a mixture of studio and live tracks. The album cover shows Elvis performing under a single bright light that could be interpreted as a stage light or star. Tracks on the album included 'Pledging My Love', 'He'll Have to Go' and 'Little Darlin''?

188. A gospel album released in February 1967 that became three times Platinum in 2010. It won a 1967 Grammy Award for Best Sacred Performance and features Elvis proudly in front of a church on the album cover. Hits on the album include 'Somebody Bigger Than You and I', 'In the Garden' and 'Crying in the Chapel'?

189. Studio album released in 1973 which has sold more than one million copies worldwide. The album cover features Elvis wearing a caped white jumpsuit passionately singing into his microphone. Tracks include 'Are you Sincere', 'Just a Little Bit' and 'Three Corn Patches'?

190. Elvis' first of three gospel albums following a lifelong love for church style music. Recorded in 1960, it was released in an attempt to give Elvis a more family-friendly image after his initial controversial start in the industry. Pictured on the sleeve cover playing a piano, the album includes the hits 'Milky White Way', 'Swing Down Sweet Chariot' and 'Mansion Over the Hilltop'.

191. Recorded in Hollywood when Elvis had recently turned 40 years old, this album featured the new rock song 'T-R-O-U-B-L-E' along with 'Fairytale', 'I Can Help' and 'And I love You So'?

192. Released in 1974 and having very minimal success, which album including the two singles 'I've Got a Thing About You Baby' and 'My Boy'?

193. Elvis' debut studio album released in March 1956 including the tracks 'Blue Suede Shoes', 'I Got a Woman' and 'Tutti Frutti'?

194. What is the name of the spoken word album released in 1974 by Colonel Tom Parker's label, Boxcar, consisting of Elvis' banter, jokes and life stories recorded in between songs from a live concert?

195. Elvis' 15th studio album released in June 1969 with the famous image of Elvis standing in front of guitar-playing silhouettes as the album cover. The final track on the album was the extremely successful 'In the Ghetto'?

196. What 1962 album features the song 'That's Someone You Never Forget', a title and concept that Elvis is rumoured to have created in memory of his late mother?

197. What live album released in October 1977 is a soundtrack to accompany a television special of the same name. It features some of Elvis' final performances from June 1977, just two months before his death?

198. Released in 1959, which album cover features Elvis in the driving seat of a car dressed in military attire?

199. Released on 8 January 1975, which album features the hit single 'If You Talk in Your Sleep'?

200. Released in October 1971, this was Elvis' second and final Christmas album and has become a festive favourite. Accompanied on most songs by The Imperial Quartet, the album included such hits as 'Winter Wonderland', 'The First Noel' and 'If I Get Home on Christmas Day'?

ANSWERS: ALBUMS

181. *Elvis Is Back!*

182. *He Touched Me*

183. *Aloha From Hawaii: Via Satellite*

184. *Love Letters from Elvis*

185. *Welcome to My World*

186. *Elvis: That's the Way It Is*

187. *Moody Blue*

188. *How Great Thou Art*

189. *Raised on Rock*

190. *His Hand in Mine*

191. *Today*

192. *Good Times*

193. *Elvis Presley*

194. *Having Fun With Elvis On Stage*

195. *From Elvis in Memphis*

196. *Pot Luck*

197. *Elvis in Concert*

198. *A Date with Elvis*

199. *Promised Land*

200. *Elvis Sings the Wonderful World of Christmas*

QUESTIONS:
FLIP SIDES

WHAT SONG WAS ON THE FLIP SIDE OF EACH OF THE FOLLOWING RELEASED SINGLES?

201. Released in 1954, what was the B-side to 'That's All Right'?

202. 'I Don't Care if the Sun Don't Shine' was the B-side to which 1954 hit?

203. 'Milkcow Blues Boogie' was the A-side, what was the B-side?

204. What was on the flip side of 'Baby Let's Play House'?

205. 'Anything That's Part of You' was the B-side to which superstitious hit?

206. 'What'd I Say' was the A-side, which huge hit was on the B-side?

207. '(It's a) Long Lonely Highway' was the B-side to which hit?

208. Which song was on the flip side of 'I Beg of You'?

209. 'Clean Up Your Own Backyard' was the A-side, which hit was the B-side?

210. 'Mystery Train' was on the flip side of which 1955 hit?

211. What was on the B-side of Moody Blue?

212. 'Almost in Love' was the A-side, what track was on the B-side?

213. Which song was on the flip side of '(You're the) Devil in Disguise'?

214. 'Thinking About You' was the B-side to which hit?

215. Which song originally by Little Richard was on the flip side of 'Blue Suede Shoes'?

216. What was on the flip side of 'Big Boss Man'?

217. '(Such an) Easy Question' was the A-side, what was the B-side?

218. 'Always on My Mind' was the B-side, what song was on the A-side?

219. 'Jailhouse Rock' was the A-side, what was the B-side?

220. Which song was on the flip side of 'If I Can Dream'?

221. 'Mr. Strongman' was the B-side to which hit?

222. What was on the B-side of 'Just Because'?

223. What was on the flip side of 'Pledging My Love'?

224. 'Long Legged Girl (With the Short Dress On)' was the A-side, what was the B-side?

225. Which romantically named hit was the B-side to 'Suspicion'?

226. Which song was on the flip side of 'Kentucky Rain'?

227. Which hit was on the B-side of 'Can't Help Falling in Love'?

228. What song was on the B-side of 'In the Ghetto'?

229. 'Do The Clam' was the A-side, what was the B-side?

230. 'Lawdy Miss Clawdy' was on the flip side of which hit?

ANSWERS:
FLIP SIDES

201. Blue Moon of Kentucky

202. Good Rockin' Tonight

203. You're a Heartbreaker

204. I'm Left, You're Right, She's Gone

205. Good Luck Charm

206. Viva Las Vegas

207. I'm Yours

208. Don't

209. The Fair is Moving On

210. I Forgot to Remember to Forget

211. She Thinks I Still Care

212. A Little Less Conversation

213. Please Don't Drag That String Around

214. My Boy

215. Tutti Frutti

216. I'm a Love You

217. It Feels So Right

218. Separate Ways

219. Treat Me Nice

220. Edge of Reality

221. T-R-O-U-B-L-E

222. Blue Moon

223. Way Down

224. That's Someone You Never Forget

225. Kiss Me Quick

226. My Little Friend

227. Rock-A-Hula Baby

228. Any Day Now

229. You'll Be Gone

230. Shake Rattle and Roll

QUESTIONS: TOP 10 SINGLES

FILL IN THE BLANKS TO REVEAL 20 OF ELVIS' TOP 10 SINGLES

231. _T'S ___ OR _____

232. __ PICI___ _IN__

233. _O_E __ _END__

234. ____K ON ___

235. S_R_E_D_R

236. _ _ _ SHO_ _ _ _

237. _O_A _O_A _A_ _

238. (_AR_ _' _H_ _A_ _) _I_ _ _TES_ _ _AM_

239. _ _ _ _ _ YOU, _ _ _ _ _ YOU, _ _ _ _ _

    YOU

240. _URN_ _ _ _O_ _

241. _ _E _O_ _ONE_ _ _ _ _O_ _ _ _ _

242. (_E_ _E_ _E _ _ _ _) _E_ _ _ _E_ _

243. _ _E _ _ _ _E_ O_ _O_

244. _EAR_ _REA_ _ _TE_

245. _O_' _R_ D_DD_

246. A _ _ _ _ _N_ _ _ _O_E

247. H_ _ _ H_ _ _ _ _ W_ _ _ _

248. _E_ _R_ _O_ _E_D_ _

249. O_ _ _I_G_T

250. _O_' B_ _R_E_

ANSWERS:
TOP 10 SINGLES

231. It's Now or Never

232. Suspicious Minds

233. Love Me Tender

234. Stuck On You

235. Surrender

236. All Shook Up

QUESTIONS: GRACELAND

251. Which American singer-songwriter who was inspired by Elvis released the album *Graceland* in 1986?

252. What is the name of the small garden at Graceland where Elvis, his parents and grandmother are buried?

253. Statues of which animal sit on the driveway wall guarding the porch at Graceland?

254. How much did Elvis pay for Graceland: $102,000, $152,000 or $202,500?

255. In what year did Elvis buy Graceland at the tender age of 22?

256. Whose visit to Graceland in 2014 prompted the tour guide to announce, "It is pretty special to have a future king take time to come visit The King"?

257. In what American State can you find Graceland?

258. Graceland is the second most visited private home in the United States. What is the first?

259. How are Furbringer and Ehrman significant names in Graceland's history?

260. In what 1984 rock music 'mockumentary' do band members gather around Elvis' grave and sing 'Heartbreak Hotel'?

261. Approximately how many visitors flock to Graceland every year: 200,000, 400,000 or 600,000?

262. In April 1976, which well-known American singer (and Elvis fan) climbed over the wall at Graceland in an attempt to meet Elvis but was intercepted by security on the front porch?

263. In what year was Graceland built: 1909, 1929 or 1939?

264. Which 2001 movie starring a host of Hollywood actors including Kurt Russell, Kevin Costner and Christian Slater told the story of a group of criminals who plan to rob a casino disguised as Elvis impersonators?

265. What is the name of the street where Graceland is located?

266. What species of large bird is immortalised in stained glass panels between the living room and music room at Graceland?

267. How many acres does the Graceland estate cover: 3.8, 13.8 or 30.8?

268. What was the name of Elvis' golden palomino quarter horse, also buried at Graceland?

269. In what year was Graceland opened to the public: 1978, 1982 or 1990?

270. Which famous singer visited Graceland in 2013 and left a guitar pick on Elvis' grave so that "Elvis can play in heaven"?

ANSWERS: GRACELAND

251. Paul Simon
252. Meditation Garden
253. Lion
254. $102,500

255. 1957

256. Prince William

257. Tennessee

258. The White House

259. They were the architects who designed Graceland

260. This Is Spinal Tap

261. 600,000

262. Bruce Springsteen

263. 1939

264. 3000 Miles to Graceland

265. Elvis Presley Boulevard (previously Highway 51 South)

266. Peacock

267. 13.8 acres

268. Rising Sun

269. 1982

270. Sir Paul McCartney

QUESTIONS:
SONGS ABOUT ELVIS

271. Which Bryan Adams song mentions many aspects of Elvis' life including Memphis, Lisa Marie, and a list of song titles?

272. Which 1979 Queen song, reportedly written by Freddie Mercury in just 10 minutes, was a tribute to Elvis?

273. 'Elvis Went to Hollywood' was a hit by which Californian rock band founded in 1991?

274. Which well-known single by electronic band Depeche Mode was inspired by Priscilla Presley's book *Elvis and Me*, according to songwriter Martin Gore?

275. 'Elvis Has Just Left the Building' was a hit for which American songwriter, musician and composer who was born in 1940 and died in 1993?

276. Which song by English singer-songwriter Elton John was a dedication to Elvis and refers to The King's birthplace in the song title?

277. Which song originally by Marc Cohn and covered by Cher features Graceland prominently and even refers to the Jungle Room?

278. What is the title of the 2005 Kate Bush song from her album *Aerial*, which questions if Elvis is actually alive and well somewhere?

279. What singer said he was devastated about Elvis' death and found the three-year process of writing 'Johnny Bye Bye' to be a great pressure?

280. What band included 'Elvis Presley and America' on their 1984 album *The Unforgettable Fire* as a reaction to Albert Goldman's unflattering biography of Elvis?

281. 'Real Good Looking Boy' was a tribute to Elvis by which British rock band, after their lead singer Roger Daltrey stated Elvis was a "Man that changed my life when I was 11. I saw Elvis Presley live at 11 and thank God I did"?

282. What is the name of the debut single by alternative rock band Bush in which singer Gavin Rossdale states that he doesn't believe that Elvis is dead?

283. 'We Remember The King' was a song by Johnny Cash featuring Carl Perkins, Roy Orbison and which other singer?

284. Mark Knopfler, most famous for being the guitarist and singer in Dire Straights released which song dedicated to 'The King of Rock and Roll'?

285. Which song by Roy Orbison that features an Elvis song in the title was included on his 1979 album *Laminar Flow*?

286. 'Lights Out' and 'Nobody Noticed It' were tributes to Elvis by which singer and actress?

287. The not so complimentary song 'DisGraceland' was released by which well-known 'shock rocker', born Vincent Furnier?

288. Which singer and friend of Elvis sang 'The Whole World Misses You (We Miss You Elvis)'?

289. Which famous Mississippi-born singer included the song 'Elvis Presley Blues' on his album *Take the Weather with You*?

290. Which Canadian singer included the track 'He Was The King' on his 27th studio album *Prairie Wind*?

ANSWERS:
SONGS ABOUT ELVIS

271. Hey Elvis
272. Crazy Little Thing Called Love
273. Counting Crows
274. Personal Jesus
275. Frank Zappa
276. Porch Swing in Tupelo
277. Walking in Memphis
278. King of the Mountain
279. Bruce Springsteen
280. U2
281. The Who
282. Everything Zen

QUESTIONS: TELEVISION SPECIALS, DOCUMENTARIES AND STAGE SHOWS

291.   Which 1960 Television special officially titled *It's Nice to Go Travelling* starred Frank Sinatra and featured Elvis in his first televised appearance since coming home from his military service in Germany?

292.   What is the name of the 1955 musical documentary film featuring Elvis that follows the career of disc jockey Bill Randle?

293.   What is the name of the 2005 Broadway jukebox musical featuring the leather-jacketed, good-looking guitar-playing character Chad?

294. Referred to as *Comeback Special*, in what year was Elvis' television special that aired following a decline in music sales?

295. Which 1972 musical documentary that followed Elvis on a 15-city tour won the Golden Globe Award for Best Documentary?

296. Which singer, who went on to become the top-selling UK singles artist of the 1980s played Elvis in *Elvis: The Musical* in 1977?

297. What is the name of the Las Vegas stage show that was created when Elvis Presley Enterprises partnered up with Cirque du Soleil to put on a musical performance at the Aria Resort and Casino?

298. What is the name of Elvis' third and final television special that was posthumously released on 3 October, 1977?

299. What is the name of the 1981 documentary based on the life of Elvis that was directed by Andrew Solt and featured pop singer Ral Donner as the narrator?

300. What is the name of the documentary by Elvis and martial arts instructor Ed Parker that follows the United States Karate team between 1973 and 1974?

ANSWERS:
TELEVISION SPECIALS,
DOCUMENTARIES AND
STAGE SHOWS

291. *Welcome Home Elvis*
292. *The Pied Piper of Cleveland: A Day in the Life of a Famous Disc Jockey*
293. *All Shook Up*
294. 1968
295. *Elvis on Tour*
296. Shakin' Stevens
297. *Viva Elvis*
298. *Elvis in Concert*
299. *This Is Elvis*
300. *The New Gladiators*

DID YOU KNOW?
200 INTERESTING ELVIS FACTS

1. In 1972 Elvis became the first solo performer to sell out Madison Square Garden for four straight shows.

2. Elvis recorded 'Always on My Mind' a few weeks after his separation from Priscilla in March 1972.

3. When Elvis enquired to Ray Peterson about the possibility of covering his track 'The Wonder of You', Peterson said, "You don't have to ask permission; you're Elvis Presley."
Elvis then replied, "Yes, I do, you're Ray Peterson."

4. Elvis' collaborator and friend J. D. Sumner could sing in an incredible double low 'C' note. According to the *Guinness Book of World Records* it is the lowest note produced by the human voice and first recorded by Sumner on his 1966 recording of the hymn 'Blessed Assurance'.

5. By the time Elvis had finished his time with the army in Germany, his friend Charlie Hodge had taught him techniques to add a full octave to his vocal range. This

enabled him to sing such songs as 'Unchained Melody' and 'I Believe'.

6. The church featured on the front cover of *How Great Thou Art* is the First Church of Christ in Sandwich, Massachusetts.

7. In 1971, it is reported that Elvis was speaking to two police officers and telling them of a restaurant that sold his favourite peanut butter, banana and bacon sandwiches. Before they knew it, they were on their way to Memphis airport and the three of them hopped on to Elvis' private jet and headed for Denver. Elvis then arranged for 22 of the sandwiches to be delivered to the plane where they were washed down with champagne before they made the two-hour return flight back to Memphis.

8. While driving through Memphis in 1967, Elvis heard Tom Jones' new song 'Green, Green Grass of Home' on the radio for the first time and loved it. He made his 'Mafia' phone the radio station multiple times so that he could hear it over and over again.

9. Elvis had blonde hair until he started dying it.

10. Elvis' autopsy revealed many drugs were present in his body when he died, including Morphine, Demerol, Chloropheniramine (anti-histamine), Placidyl (tranquilizer), Valium, Codeine, Ethinamate, Quaaludes and barbiturates.

11. Elvis was reluctant to have The Beatles as guests at his Bel Air mansion in 1965 due to their open drug-taking and anti-Vietnam political views. After an apparent awkward silence however, the meeting was a laughter-filled occasion.

12. Frank Sinatra once described Elvis' singing style as, "The most brutal, ugly, degenerate, vicious form of expression it has been my displeasure to hear...it is sung, played and written, for the most part, by cretinous goons."

13. Elvis owned more than 40 guns including m-16s and a Thomson sub-machinegun.

14. Some of Elvis' jumpsuits weighed more than two stones.

15. In 1965, Elvis thought about entering a monastery.

16. In high school, Elvis' music teacher told him that he couldn't sing and gave him a C-grade.

17. One of Elvis' girlfriends, Peggy Lipton, claimed that Elvis was impotent due to his frequent drug use.

18. Blues legend B.B. King said he used to play in the blues clubs of Beale Street with a pre-famous Elvis in the early 1950s.

19. It is estimated that Elvis was prescribed 10,000 pills the year he died.

20. Food served at Elvis and Priscilla's wedding included oysters, clams, salmon, lobster, fried chicken and a wedding cake that cost $3,500.

21. *Elvis: The Musical* featured three different actors playing Elvis in any one performance; one for the early years, one for the army and movie star years and one for the Las Vegas years.

22. Elvis was given a guitar for his 11th birthday. He wasn't very happy though – he really wanted a bicycle.

23. Elvis' pets included several horses, donkeys,

peacocks, a Pomeranian, ducks, chickens, a turkey, various dog breeds, a chimpanzee, a monkey and a mynah bird.

24. Elvis liked to collect marble statues, particularly of the Venus de Milo and Joan of Arc.

25. Michael Jackson once said to his then wife, Lisa Marie Presley, "I am afraid that I am going to end up like Elvis and die the way he did."

26. Elvis' ancestry is Scottish, Irish, German, Welsh, French and Cherokee Indian.

27. After Elvis' funeral, there was a public viewing of the casket at Graceland with over 30,000 fans allowed in to see his body.

28. Elvis became 'practically evangelical' about the benefits of amphetamines after being introduced to them during his time in the army.

29. Elvis was a direct descendant of Abraham Lincoln's great-great grandfather, Isaiah Harrison.

30. In his final days, Elvis would sit and recite his

favourite Monty Python sketches.

31. For the 1981 documentary *This Is Elvis*, pop singer Ral Donner imitated Elvis' voice for the narration.

32. In 1988, 'Hound Dog' was named the most played record of all time on American Juke Boxes.

33. Elvis' famous 'shaky legs' were apparently due to stage fright initially. He would over-exaggerate the movements to hide his nerves.

34. During a concert at Nassau Coliseum in 1975, Elvis threw a guitar into the audience and said, "Whoever got the guitar can keep the damn thing. I don't need it anyway."

35. Sheet-metal worker Louis Balint punched Elvis after he claimed that his wife's love for the singer had caused their relationship to break down. Balint was fined $19.60 but was jailed because he was unable to pay the fine.

36. In 1938, when Elvis was three-years-old, his dad Vernon was imprisoned for eight years for falsifying a cheque.

37. Elvis moved to Memphis when he was 13-years-old.

38. Colonel Tom Parker sold 'I Hate Elvis' badges to make money from those who wouldn't otherwise buy Elvis' music or merchandise.

39. Elvis was emotionally distraught when actor James Dean died in 1955.

40. Elvis rented out the entire top floor of the New York Hilton Hotel when he played Madison Square Garden in 1972.

41. Elvis only ever endorsed one product in his lifetime and that was Texas-based Southern Maid Doughnuts.

42. It is claimed that when he was in his 20s, Elvis could eat eight cheeseburgers and three milkshakes for lunch.

43. Due to his energetic early stage performances, Elvis would lose several pounds during a concert.

44. Natalie Wood, a brief 1956 girlfriend of Elvis, once said of his bedroom performance, "He can sing but he can't do much else."

45. After recording 'If I Can Dream', Elvis was so exhausted he collapsed.

46. Elvis would often sign autographs on fan's breasts – 'Elvis' on the left and 'Presley' on the right.

47. The idea for Elvis to wear more flamboyant outfits during his concerts came from Liberace.

48. A boyhood friend of Elvis' claimed he would put a cardboard tube in his pants while performing.

49. Elvis was an insomniac.

50. Elvis hated fish as a meal and wouldn't allow Priscilla to eat it at Graceland.

51. Rolling Stone magazine named Elvis the third greatest musical artist of all time behind The Beatles and Bob Dylan.

52. Before he managed Elvis, Colonel Tom Parker toured with an act called The Dancing Chickens where he would rather cruelly put chickens on a red-hot plate to give the impression that they were having a boogie.

53. Elvis was originally considered for the role of Tony in the musical West Side Story. A part that eventually went to Richard Beymer.

54. *Elvis Presley*, Elvis' debut album was the first rock and roll album to make it to the top of the charts.

55. Elvis' last words spoken in public were reportedly to his assistant regarding a forthcoming concert tour, "Billy, son, this is gonna be my best tour ever."

56. The day before he died, Elvis tried to obtain a print of *Star Wars: Episode IV – A New Hope*, for Lisa Marie.

57. Elvis believed he would die in his 40s like his mother.

58. In 1977, the year that Elvis died, he was the top touring act in the United States.

59. Elvis wore a chai necklace because his great-grandmother was Jewish. He said, "I don't want to miss out on going to heaven on a technicality."

60. In the mid-1970s, the kitchen at Graceland was kept open 24 hours a day. Apparently the busiest time was at

about 4.30 a.m. when Elvis would get a craving for burgers or peanut butter and banana sandwiches.

61. James Brown was one of three of the only famous people who attended Elvis' funeral. The others were George Hamilton and Ann-Margret.

62. When Elvis met President Nixon in 1970, Nixon said to Elvis, "You dress kind of strange, don't you?" To which Elvis replied, "Well, Mr. President, you got your show and I got mine."

63. Elvis is a member of the Country Music Hall of Fame, the Gospel Music Hall of Fame, the Rockabilly Hall of Fame and the Rock and Roll Hall of Fame.

64. It is thought that Elvis was six months away from bankruptcy when he died.

65. Elvis' nicknames included 'The Memphis Flash', 'Big E', 'The King of Western Bop' and 'The Chief'.

66. On stage, Elvis often referred to the song 'Fairytale' as the story of his life.

67. Every time Ann-Margret opened a show in Las

Vegas, Elvis would send her flowers arranged in a guitar shape.

68. Elvis loved eating burnt bacon.

69. Television host Ed Sullivan once declared Elvis 'unfit for family viewing' due to his public thrusting.

70. Elvis loved to play Monopoly.

71. The BBC refused to pay for Elvis' 1972 concert Aloha From Hawaii and so it was not shown in the United Kingdom.

72. Elvis' mum Gladys' middle name was Love.

73. Elvis didn't individually write any of his song releases and has very few song writing credits at all.

74. Eddie Murphy credits Elvis as the person who inspired him to pursue a career in show business.

75. Elvis' final concert performance was in Indianapolis, Indiana, on 26 June, 1977.

76. All three of Elvis' Grammy Awards were for his

gospel music.

77. Singer Liam Gallagher has a tattoo of The Memphis Mafia's logo 'TCB' on his right arm in tribute to Elvis.

78. Elvis' favourite toothpaste brand was Colgate.

79. Elvis preferred to bath using just a rag and some soap.

80. Elvis took 31 takes before he was happy with his recording for 'Hound Dog'.

81. As a teenager, Elvis would style his hair using Vaseline.

82. Elvis has had 130 UK hit singles and 21 UK number 1 singles.

83. After Elvis' stepmother had replaced some Graceland furniture and curtains that Elvis' mother had chosen, Elvis angrily loaded a removal van with all of her possessions including household goods, clothes and pets. He then moved her and his dad, Vernon, out of Graceland into a new house on Dolan Drive, which borders the Graceland estate.

84. When Robert Plant and John Paul Jones from Led Zeppelin met Elvis in 1973, Elvis swapped his $5000 gold watch with Jones' $15 Mickey Mouse one.

85. At a Chicago auction in 2009, a lock of Elvis' hair fetched $18,300. Although it was never DNA tested, it was certified authentic by a 'celebrity hair expert'.

86. Because Elvis was still classed as a minor when he signed to RCA in 1955, aged just 20, his dad Vernon had to sign the contract for him.

87. The word Elvisology is the official term for historical and statistical information on the life and career of Elvis.

88. The 1998 film *Finding Graceland* stars Harvey Keitel as an Elvis impersonator pretending to be the real Elvis in an attempt to hitch a ride to Memphis.

89. Elvis' favourite form of martial arts was American Kenpo.

90. It is estimated that, at the time of Elvis' death, there were approximately 170 Elvis Presley impersonators. Today, there could be as many as 250,000.

91. In 1953 after Elvis' first visit to Sun Records, receptionist Marion Keisker made a note for label boss Sam Phillips: 'Good ballad singer. Hold'.

92. Elvis' last meal was thought to be ice cream and cookies.

93. The translation of the name 'Elvis' in Norse is 'All wise'.

94. Elvis was turned down when he auditioned for a spot on talent television show *Arthur Godfrey's Talent Scouts* in 1955.

95. An inspiration for Elvis' trademark look, which included a quiff hairstyle and jumpsuit was a comic book hero called Captain Marvel Jr.

96. There is an Elvis themed lounge at Prestwick Airport in Glasgow, Scotland.

97. Elvis was almost killed when he was 15 months old during a Mississippi tornado.

98. Elvis worked as a truck driver but disliked it so started taking evening classes in the hope of becoming

an electrician.

99. Both Bela Lugosi and Babe Ruth also died on 16 August, just in different years.

100. Singers influenced by Elvis after seeing him perform live when they were growing up include Bruce Springsteen, Roy Orbison and Cher.

101. Elvis' tombstone reads 'Elvis Aaron Presley' although he was born 'Elvis Aron Presley'. This is because Elvis wanted his middle name to be the same as Aaron from the Bible.

102. Elvis' debut single 'That's All Right/Blue Moon of Kentucky' sold 6,000 copies before it was even released due to a mass of pre-orders following its first play on Memphis radio station WHBQ in July 1954.

103. In a survey, Elvis was the eighth most popular name for pet dogs in the UK.

104. The album Promised Land was released on Elvis' 40th birthday (8 January 1975).

105. Elvis holds the record for the third most Billboard

number 1 hits with 17, after Mariah Carey (18) and The Beatles (20).

106. After a one-night stand with Marilyn Monroe in 1956, Elvis reportedly said, "She's a nice gal, but a little tall for me."

107. According to Elvis' official website, the role of Danny Fisher in King Creole was his personal favourite.

108. Elvis' movie idol was Tony Curtis.

109. Elvis gave names to his trademark jumpsuits, including Gypsy and Mad Tiger.

110. Elvis very rarely drank alcohol after witnessing family members become alcoholics.

111. In 1961, Elvis put on a concert and raised more than $50,000 for the completion of a Hawaiian memorial to those who were killed on the USS Arizona during the 1941 Pearl Harbour attack.

112. The 2004 American jukebox musical *All Shook Up* is based on William Shakespeare's 1602 play, *Twelfth Night*.

113. Elvis was nicknamed 'Elvis the Pelvis' due to his trademark hip movement on stage.

114. Elvis kept a grocery list of items that he wanted to be stocked at Graceland at all times. Among the items were cigarettes, cigars, pickles, pepsi, banana pudding, bacon, shredded coconut, biscuits and a laxative gum called Feen-a-Mint.

115. Elvis met The Beach Boys' Brian Wilson in 1975 but the meeting ended badly after Wilson made a karate move on Elvis even though Elvis had requested him not to.

116. Elvis had a slight stutter.

117. Elvis once used black shoe polish to dye his hair.

118. A critic labelled one of Elvis' first concerts 'a jug of corn liquor at a champagne party'.

119. In between filming Love Me Tender in 1956 and *Loving You* in 1957, Elvis had his nose done, his teeth capped and his acne treated.

120. Elvis always wanted to play Marlon Brando's

character Don Corleone in The Godfather but was never considered for the role.

121. Elvis once spent two years eating nothing but meatloaf, tomatoes and mashed potato.

122. Elvis once spotted a petrol station attendant being attacked by two youths and so he jumped out of his limo and took up a karate stance. The shock of being confronted by Elvis stopped the youths being violent.

123. Every song on Elvis' debut album *Elvis Presley* was released as a single.

124. Kurt Russell played Elvis in the 1971 film *Elvis* and was also the voice of Elvis in the 1994 film Forrest Gump.

125. During Elvis' first major tour, an outraged Christian wrote to the FBI warning that Elvis was a security risk: 'Elvis Presley is a definite danger to the security of the United States…His actions and motions were such as to rouse the sexual passions of teenaged youth'.

126. Grenada was the first country to put Elvis' face on

a stamp.

127. For his 36th birthday, Elvis treated himself to police equipment.

128. According to Priscilla, Elvis hated the plots of his movie musicals but enjoyed the millions of dollars they brought in.

129. Parents weren't impressed after Elvis' sexualised television performances. A 14-year-old girl told the media, "My parents locked up my Elvis records and broke my record player."

130. In 1973, Elvis overdosed on barbiturates spending three days in a coma.

131. Elvis collected police badges and acquired one from almost every city he sang in.

132. Some people claim that Colonel Tom Parker could hypnotize Elvis.

133. When Elvis was a child, his family were very poor and relied on government assistance.

134. When singing 'Love Me Tender' during *Elvis: The '68 Comeback Special* and knowing that Priscilla was in the audience, Elvis jokingly sang 'You have made my life a wreck' instead of 'You have made my life complete'.

135. The National Guard was called in to provide security at some of Elvis' early concerts.

136. Due to strict Islamic laws, Elvis impersonators in Mogadishu, Somalia, are required to have beards.

137. Elvis was a sleepwalker in his youth.

138. In the army, Elvis was honoured by his commanding officer for his 'cheerfulness, drive and continually outstanding leadership ability'.

139. Other actors who have played Elvis on the big screen include Don Johnson (*Elvis and the Beauty Queen*, 1981), Bruce Campbell (*Bubba Ho-Tep*, 2002), Jonathan Rhys Meyers (*Elvis*, 2005) and Frank Stallone (*Angels with Angles*, 2005).

140. Elvis used A&D ointment to keep his lips soft.

141. In 1997, a report showed that Elvis was the world's

bestselling posthumous entertainer with worldwide sales of over one billion.

142. There are over 480 active Elvis fan clubs.

143. Viva Elvis, the Las Vegas stage show performed by Cirque du Soleil only ran from 2010 to 2012 due to low attendances.

144. Elvis has spent over 1170 weeks in the UK singles chart.

145. Mobs in some US cities even burned effigies of Elvis believing him to be a bad role model.

146. It is thought that Elvis' voice spanned three octaves.

147. Colonel Tom Parker took as much as 50% in commission from Elvis' earnings.

148. An estimated 250,000 UK fans still buy Elvis records.

149. Elvis topped the scales at more than 250lbs in later life.

150. At a meeting with rocker Alice Cooper in a Las Vegas hotel suite, Elvis pulled out a loaded gun and told Cooper to point it at him, as he would teach him how to disarm a gunman. Cooper jokingly said for a split-second he thought about shooting Elvis and always be remembered as the guy who did so. Before he had time to think however, Cooper was on the floor with Elvis' boot on his throat.

151. The Clash's 1979 album cover for *London Calling* was styled on the album cover for Elvis' debut album Elvis Presley.

152. In 1964, Elvis paid $55,000 for a 165-foot yacht that once belonged to President Franklin D. Roosevelt. Elvis didn't keep it for long and donated it to St. Jude's Children's Hospital for them to sell and raise much needed funds.

153. Outside the gates of Graceland at Elvis' funeral, a car ploughed into a group of fans killing two women and critically injuring a third.

154. Elvis lived on a street named after him while he was still alive.

155. As a two-year-old, Elvis broke the grasp of his mother's hand and ran to sing with the choir during an 'Assembly of God' church service.

156. Elvis once asked his limo driver, "Do you own this limo or do you work for the company?"
He responded, "I work for the company."
Elvis said, "Well, you own it now," and bought the limo for him.

157. In 1958, 'Hound Dog' exceeded three million copies in the United States becoming only the third single to do so after Bing Crosby's 'White Christmas' and Gene Autry's 'Rudolph The Red Nose Reindeer'.

158. After being threatened with kidnap and assassination, Elvis always performed with a pistol in each of his boots.

159. Elvis was extremely generous and would give personal possessions away to family and even strangers who showed any admiration towards him.

160. Nobody knows the exact number of songs Elvis recorded during his long career but it could potentially be as many as 1,200.

161. In Switzerland it is illegal to cut a front lawn dressed as Elvis.

162. Elvis was a member of his high school's boxing team.

163. Some unusually titled songs that Elvis recorded include '(There's) No Room to Rhumba in a Sports Car', 'Yoga is as Yoga Does' and 'Queenie Wahini's Papaya'.

164. The National Rifle Association created an 'Elvis Presley Tribute Revolver' in 2007.

165. Elvis' informal jamming in front of a small audience in the television special *Elvis: The '68 Comeback Special* is thought to be the forerunner of the 'unplugged' concept, now popular on many music channels.

166. An indoor waterfall, a jungle room, music-themed iron entrance gates and a racquetball building can be found at Graceland.

167. Four separate psychics told actor Patrick Swayze that Elvis was his guardian angel.

168. A 1955 article in *Country Song Roundup* magazine described Elvis as a 'folk music fireball'.

169. Elvis was awarded two medals during his time in the army, one for expert marksmanship and the other for sharpshooting.

170. Elvis smoked thin German cigars.

171. In 2006, George W. Bush became the first sitting United States President to visit Graceland. He went with Japanese Prime Minister, Junichiro Koizumi.

172. When he was a boy, Elvis broke another child's hip during a wrestling match.

173. Elvis' favourite American Football team was The Cleveland Browns.

174. In the 1970s, Elvis would start concerts with 'Also Sprach Zarathustra', which is the theme tune for the 1968 movie 2001: A Space Odyssey.

175. Elvis became the first rock and roll singer to be honoured by the United States Postal Service with a commemorative stamp.

176. When Elvis made his final appearance on Ed Sullivan's show in 1957, censors demanded that he could only be filmed from the waist up.

177. *The Pied Piper of Cleveland: A Day in the Life of a Famous Disc Jockey*, a 1955 American musical documentary was the first film that Elvis appeared in.

178. Elvis stood at six feet tall.

179. Muhammad Ali once gave Elvis boxing gloves with 'You're the Greatest' on.

180. Elvis became a karate black belt in 1960 and incorporated karate moves in his performances.

181. Graceland was built by Dr. Thomas Moore and his wife Ruth on land that was once part of a 500-acre farm called Graceland in honour of the original owner's daughter, Grace.

182. A version of 'Are You Lonesome Tonight?' known as the 'Laughing Version' in which Elvis breaks into fits of laughter throughout the song made the UK charts after his death.

183. Elvis never learned to read music.

184. In the early 1970s, Elvis would drive around and pull people over whilst pretending to be a police officer. Instead of giving out tickets, he would give out autographs.

185. In 2006, Graceland became a recognised United States National Historic Landmark.

186. 'Elvis' is one of the most popular computer passwords.

187. Colonel Tom Parker was an illegal immigrant from The Netherlands but pretended to be from West Virginia. His true origins and real name (Andreas Cornelis van Kuijk) weren't public knowledge until sometime during the 1980s.

188. Elvis dyed his eyelashes black, which caused eye problems later in life.

189. On The Steve Allen Show, Elvis sang 'Hound Dog' to a Basset Hound.

190. Original copies of *Good Times*, with a sticker on the

cover stating the singles on the album, are very rare and reach big money at auctions.

191. Elvis was smitten with *Bewitched* star Elizabeth Montgomery.

192. Elvis often visited a Memphis morgue to look at corpses.

193. Elvis' favourite aftershave brand was Brut.

194. The Germans called Elvis 'The Rock and Roll Matador'.

195. Some people consider Elvis' 1954 single 'That's All Right (Mama)' to be the first ever rock and roll record.

196. Elvis has four Grandchildren.

197. Elvis never sang 'Viva Las Vegas' live.

198. When Ed Sullivan eventually gave in and invited Elvis on to his television show in 1956, it drew an audience of 72 million – one third of America's population.

199. Elvis' 1970 meeting with President Nixon was kept secret until *The Washington Post* broke the story about a year later.

200. When Elvis visited President Nixon in 1970, he brought a number of gifts with him including a Colt 45 pistol.

ABOUT THE AUTHOR

Scott Stevenson is an author, actor and artist. He was born in Bath in 1983 and grew up in rural surroundings and has a bachelor's degree in Environmental Science from Bath Spa University.

After spending a number of years managing a team supporting children and young adults on the autistic spectrum, Scott followed his dream of working in the film and television industry. To date, he has appeared in over 200 productions including music videos for *Kasabian* and *The Kaiser Chiefs*, various television commercials and featured roles in successful movies such as *Les Miserables, Muppets Most Wanted, Mission: Impossible – Rogue Nation* and *The Imitation Game*. In addition, his work on television includes well-loved series, most notably *Doctor Who, Downton Abbey* and *EastEnders* to name but a few.

Scott also paints commissioned artwork, writes children's stories and likes to watch his beloved Liverpool FC play. He also participates in local pub quizzes across Somerset and frequently composes quiz questions for social functions. Scott lives in Midsomer Norton in Somerset, where he enjoys spending time with his young family and coaching a local children's football team.

www.apexpublishing.co.uk

Printed in May 2022
by Rotomail Italia S.p.A., Vignate (MI) - Italy